COLLISION
COURSE

Nigel Hinton

HIT PLAYS

THE FWOG PWINCE by Kaye Umansky
BILL'S NEW FROCK by Anne Fine
THE COMPUTER NUT by Betsy Byars
COLLISION COURSE by Nigel Hinton
MAID MARIAN AND HER MERRY MEN
   by Tony Robinson

Series Editors

Robin Little
Patrick Redsell
Erik Wilcock

CONTENTS

This drama was first produced in the Scene series on BBC School Television in 1991 and was produced and directed by Roger Tonge.

Introduction

Collision Course, adapted by Nigel Hinton from his novel, is one of the **Hit Plays**. All of the books in the series have been produced for either television or radio.

The plays are very much in the form they were in when they were first recorded. This play relies quite heavily on camera directions and these have been edited so that they can be spoken dramatically by two narrators.

The plays in the series are for readers aged 11–13. This does not mean that all of them are the same in any way; they are as varied as the people who will study them as part of their reading programme for Key Stage 3 in English. The one thing the plays have in common is that they are enjoyable to read.

On the next page you will find a section entitled 'What the play is about'. This summarises the action in the play as well as focusing on some of the main issues dealt with in it. Following this, there is a section called 'Preparing for reading'. This gives the information you need to read the play successfully. There are brief descriptions of the characters, who they are and how much they have to say.

At the end of the book there are two sections which outline some activities you can do after you have read the play. 'Drama activities' (page 56) provides clearly organised ways of getting to grips with the script and how it works in production. 'Writing and talking about the play' (page 58) gives some straight-forward assignments to help you in your understanding of the play.

What the play is about

Ray is sitting at home one evening doing homework. When he gets bored and decides to go out for a walk, he cannot possibly foresee the consequences of his actions. He sees a motorbike in a pub car park and in a moment of madness, he decides to steal it. The exhilaration of riding the bike turns to horror as he runs into a woman standing by her car on a lonely country road. When he realises that the woman is dead, he panics and runs off through the woods.

Ray's life takes on the qualities of a nightmare as he keeps imagining the scene of the crash. Quite ordinary things that people say become important because they remind him of the terrible thing that he has done. Even when he gets into the football team as reserve, and starts going out with a girl he likes, his good luck seems hollow, when he thinks about the death that he has caused.

As a background to Ray's personal tragedy, there is the serious illness of his grandmother. When he goes to see her in the hospital, he tries to confess what he has done, but she has already fallen asleep under the influence of the drugs that she is taking, and does not hear him.

This play is a fascinating exploration of the state of mind of Ray, an ordinary boy who becomes extraordinary because of the enormity of the thing that he has done. The crime was his own fault, yet there is the feeling that Fate has drawn him into a web of circumstances from which he cannot in the end escape.

Preparing for reading

This play is written in very straightforward language and should not present too many problems. There are twenty-nine speaking parts, ten females and nineteen males, plus two narrators who have the job of setting the scene and describing characters' thoughts, feelings and reactions to events. They have the two largest speaking parts. At the beginning of each scene, the characters who appear in it are listed.

The action of the play takes in a variety of locations and covers a time span of several days. Since the play is dealing with the plight of a schoolboy, the interaction he has with his family and school will be easily recognisable to most pupils.

Character	Description	Role
NARRATOR 1	narrator	large
NARRATOR 2	narrator	large
RAY	main character	large
DAD	Ray's dad	medium
MUM	Ray's mother	medium
DEREK	Ray's brother	small
DAVE	school boy	medium
JANE	school girl	medium
BARBARA	school girl	small
ANNA	school girl	medium
IAN	school boy	small
DOUGIE	school boy	small
PATRICIA	school girl	small
MR HAWKS	school teacher	small
MRS SCOTT	French teacher	small

Character	Description	Role
MR RAINES	P. E. teacher	small
CAPTAIN	footballer	small
H7	winger	small
REF	football referee	small
CHRIS	school boy	small
MRS CHALMERS	school governor	small
GRANDMA	Ray's grandma	small
MRS FITZROY	family friend	small
NURSE	hospital nurse	small
CONDUCTOR	bus conductor	small
ANNOUNCER	radio voice	small
INSPECTOR	policeman	small
ACTOR	film actor	small
ACTRESS	film actress	small
VOICE	telephone voice	small
MAN	passer-by	small

This play can be read around the class and has enough parts to involve everybody. The roles of the narrators are very important and should be read dramatically. They can really heighten the dramatic situations. This is particularly true in the flashback and nightmare sequences.

The play can also be read in groups of five or six. There are never more than eight characters in one scene. As long as the readers for Narrator 1, Narrator 2 and Ray remain constant, the others can negotiate the rest of the reading themselves on a scene-by-scene basis.

To get you started

Before you start reading this play here is an issue that you might like to discuss. Look at the details of the following crimes:

- Duggie Preston works as a bouncer at the 'Room At The Top'. While trying to evict a customer from the club, he managed to break the customer's skull.

- Ethel Baker was caught leaving the check-out at the local supermarket with three tins of cat food, a loaf of bread and a bottle of milk which she had shop-lifted.

- Albert Starling is a computer hacker who sells lists of names to companies who wish to sell products through the post. He also supplies information from computers to private detective agencies.

Now discuss the three crimes and put them into an order of seriousness with the most serious number one and the least serious number three.

Next imagine that you have been asked to find a suitable punishment for each of these offenders. Discuss what other information you would like to know about the person who has committed the crime before you felt able to give them a fair punishment. Would there be circumstances which would make you give a lenient punishment? Would there be circumstances that would make you harsh in your punishment?

The play you are about to read centres around a crime. As you read the play think about the circumstances which surround the crime and think how you would treat the character who commits the crime.

Collision Course

ACT ONE

Scene 1: Ray's bedroom, evening
(NARRATORS 1 and 2 and RAY)

NARRATOR 1   Ray is sitting at his desk doing some work. After a moment he stops and yawns. He's feeling bored. He flips the books shut and pushes them away. After switching on the radio, he walks round the room and looks at himself in the mirror. He goes back to the radio where the music has stopped and a DJ is talking.

RAY   Aw, shut up. Yak, yak.

NARRATOR 2   Ray switches off the radio and looks out of the window at the dark street outside. Suddenly the light bulb crackles and goes out, leaving just the desk light on. Ray looks up at it. Then he pulls his parka and scarf off the back of the door and starts to put them on.

Scene 2: Downstairs corridor, evening
(NARRATORS 1 and 2, MUM, DAD and RAY)

NARRATOR 1   In the kitchen, Ray's mother is on the phone. She is pacing backwards and forwards in an agitated way.

3

MUM	Yes, I'm sure it is, Doctor...I was just wondering if it would....No, I know that...Yes...I understand...
NARRATOR 2	Along the corridor Ray is tiptoeing down the stairs. He looks towards the kitchen, then glances into the sitting room where his young brother Derek is watching TV. He opens the front door and jumps as he comes face to face with his father.
DAD	Ray!
RAY	Hi, Dad.
DAD	Where you off to?
RAY	Oh, just a quick walk. Need a bit of air.
DAD	It's getting chilly. See you later, Ray.
RAY	Won't be long.
NARRATOR 1	Ray steps out, his father steps in.
RAY	My bulb's blown.
NARRATOR 2	Dad acknowledges this with a look, then a nod. The door closes.

Scene 3: City streets, night
(NARRATORS 1 and 2)

NARRATOR 1	Ray is sitting on a wall watching the traffic go by. He gets up and walks past a laundrette. There are a couple of people sitting forlornly near the machines.

4

NARRATOR 2	Ray walks on. He hears the roar of a motorbike. He stops and watches the bike go by.
NARRATOR 1	The rider pulls in to a pub car park. He gets off the bike, puts it on its rest and goes into the pub, leaving the engine running.
NARRATOR 2	Ray walks over to the bike. He runs his hands over the handlebars. He glances towards the pub. He bends forward, in imitation of a rider at speed. He glances towards the pub again and then makes a decision. He slips the bike off the stand, puts it into gear and moves away. He wobbles a bit, then roars into the night.

Scene 4: City streets, night
(NARRATORS 1 and 2)

NARRATOR 1	Ray comes to a roundabout. He goes round it and takes the exit to Blackston. It's a dark country road.
NARRATOR 2	He feels the exhilaration of this adventure. He whoops out loud and does a couple of wiggles on the bike.

Scene 5: Blackston Road, night
(NARRATORS 1 and 2, RAY and MRS·CHALMERS)

NARRATOR 1	Ray slows the bike and stops. He's cold. He wraps the scarf round his neck and zips the

parka up. Just as he finishes this, headlights shine on his face.

NARRATOR 2   He looks down, pretending to fiddle with something on the bike. To his horror, the car slows and stops. A sixty-three year old lady in a feathery hat calls from the mini.

MRS CHALMERS   Excuse me. Did you notice if the petrol station near the round-about was open?

RAY   Sorry.

MRS CHALMERS   I think I'm nearly out of petrol. Oh well, just have to hope for the best.

NARRATOR 1   Ray puts the bike into gear quickly and rather jerkily rides off up the darkened road.

Scene 6: Country lane, night
(NARRATORS 1 and 2 and RAY)

NARRATOR 1   Ray comes over the crest and swings into a turn which takes him back the way he came. He stops, legs astride the bike, and looks down at the distant lights of the town. He's panting with exhilaration and there's a smile on his face. Suddenly he becomes aware of what he's done. The smile fades.

RAY   You – are – crazy.
Crazy. What are you up to?
You'd better get out of this mess quick.

6

NARRATOR 2	He looks back at the town. He puts the bike into gear and heads off down the hill, back towards the town.

Scene 7: Blackston Road, night

(NARRATORS 1 and 2 and RAY)

NARRATOR 1	Ray speeds down the road.
NARRATOR 2	Mrs Chalmers sits in her mini.
NARRATOR 1	Ray speeds down the road.
NARRATOR 2	Mrs Chalmers turns the key, trying in vain to start the engine.
NARRATOR 1	Ray approaches a bend.
NARRATOR 2	He takes the bend, then sees the interior light of the mini as Mrs Chalmers starts to get out of the car. Ray slams on the brakes and the bike skids.
NARRATOR 1	The bike careers towards Mrs Chalmers as Ray falls off. The bike continues on its way and smashes into her.
NARRATOR 2	There is the terrible noise of metal on tarmac, of breaking glass, and the soft crump of a human body onto the ground.
NARRATOR 1	Then silence.
NARRATOR 2	Ray drags himself to his feet. Slowly he approaches Mrs Chalmers' dead body.

RAY	Oh God.
NARRATOR 1	He leans closer and touches her pulse. As he feels the stillness of death, he gasps and darts back in horror.
NARRATOR 2	A sound in the distance catches Ray's ear. A long way away the lights of an oncoming car begin to light up the road. Ray snatches up his scarf from the ground, runs to the bike and quickly rubs his scarf over the handlebars in an attempt to eradicate his fingerprints. Then, with the car getting terrifyingly closer and louder, he dashes off into the wood at the side of the road.

Scene 8: Blackston Road, night

(NARRATORS 1 and 2 and MAN)

NARRATOR 1	Like a frightened deer, Ray runs through the woods, brushing branches aside.
NARRATOR 2	Meanwhile, a car stops near the accident. A man and a woman start to get out of the car.
NARRATOR 1	The man approaches the body. The woman is behind him. The man bends over and peers at the face.
MAN	It's Mrs Chalmers.
NARRATOR 2	The woman screams.

Scene 9: Bus shelter, night

(NARRATORS 1 and 2 and RAY)

NARRATOR 1   Ray crouches in a corner of the bus shelter. His jeans are torn and there is blood on his knee. There's the sound of a police siren and Ray hides as a police car races by, followed by an ambulance. Ray's face crumples with fear and misery. He's close to tears. His hands cover his face.

RAY   Oh God. Oh God.

NARRATOR 2   A bus draws up. Ray looks up in fear. Someone gets off. Ray pulls the parka hood over his head, gets on, and goes upstairs.

Scene 10: On the bus, night

(NARRATORS 1 and 2, RAY and CONDUCTOR)

NARRATOR 1   Ray sits alone on the upper deck of the bus, staring ahead.

NARRATOR 2   The conductor reaches the top of the stairs and moves down the aisle towards him. Ray quickly pulls the parka hood further down over his face. He starts to fumble in his pockets for money. Another police car goes by, siren screaming. The conductor watches it go by.

CONDUCTOR   Must be something up.

RAY   I'm sorry, I must've left my money at home.

CONDUCTOR   Oh yeah, I've heard all that before.

RAY	It's true. Look, I'm sorry, I'll get off.
NARRATOR 1	Ray gets up and goes towards the stairs. The conductor grabs his arm and pulls him round. He looks full in his face before Ray can duck his head.
CONDUCTOR	It's a bit late now, isn't it, now you've done it.
RAY	I haven't done anything.
CONDUCTOR	You've had your ride, haven't you? Go on, get off.
NARRATOR 2	The conductor lets go and Ray starts down the stairs.
NARRATOR 1	The bus pulls up. Ray starts to get off.
CONDUCTOR	I won't forget you.
NARRATOR 2	Ray gets off the bus and limps away.

Scene 11: Ray's road, night
(NARRATORS 1 and 2 and MUM'S VOICE)

NARRATOR 1	Ray comes limping along the road. He stops at the garden gate and looks up the path to the front door.
NARRATOR 2	Suddenly, disturbing pictures flash through Ray's mind. He imagines that two policemen are standing at the open front door talking to his mother. She looks past them to Ray and cries out in anguish.

MUM'S VOICE	Ray, Ray. What've you done?
NARRATOR 1	Ray comes back to reality. He walks up to the door and quietly slips the key in the lock.

Scene 12: The hallway
(NARRATORS 1 and 2)

NARRATOR 1	Ray tiptoes up the stairs. There's a loud creak. He stops a moment, then starts up again.
NARRATOR 2	He makes it to his bedroom without being seen.

Scene 13: Ray's bedroom, night
(NARRATORS 1 and 2, DAD and RAY)

NARRATOR 1	Ray takes off his parka, shoes and jeans, trying to avoid hurting his cut knee. He gets the jeans off and grabs some tissues from the top of his chest of drawers. He sits on the bed and starts to dab at the cut.
NARRATOR 2	In his mind he hears the roar of the motorbike ending in a loud crash. He sees Mrs Chalmers lying dead on the road.
NARRATOR 1	There's a knock at his door.
DAD	Ray... Ray...

RAY	Yeah, OK. Hold on.
NARRATOR 2	Ray rumples his bed to make it look as if he's been asleep. Then he unlocks the door.
DAD	You in bed already?
RAY	Thought I'd have an early night.
DAD	Didn't even know you were back.
RAY	I was only out for about ten minutes. Then I did some work.
DAD	Ray... We've had some bad news about Grandma. She's been taken into hospital. It looks serious. Your Mum's going to be a bit... well, you know – things'll be a bit difficult. So do all you can to make things as smooth as possible. I know I can count on you.
RAY	Yeah.
DAD	Have to put a new bulb in. You all right?
RAY	Yeah.
DAD	Sure? You'd tell me if anything was wrong, wouldn't you?
RAY	'Course. There's nothing. I'm just sad about Grandma.
DAD	Yeah, well... bad things happen. Anyway, 'night son.
RAY	'Night.

NARRATOR 1	As his Dad walks away, Ray closes the door. He leans his back against it. His face crumples with the fear and loneliness.
RAY	Dad. Help me.

Scene 14: Dream sequence
(NARRATORS 1 and 2)

NARRATOR 1	School. A long line of pupils stretches out across the playground. They are all dressed in white shirts or blouses and dark trousers or skirts. Ray is standing among them wearing a dark shirt and white trousers. He stands out hopelessly. A detective and a uniformed policeman are leading the bus conductor along the line. As they arrive at each pupil, the pupils step forward and hold out their hands for inspection.
NARRATOR 2	Ray's turn comes. He steps forward. The long line of pupils turn and look at him. His mother, father and Derek are also in the dream, in a little separate group. Ray holds out his hands. They are covered in blood. His mother howls in misery while her husband holds her.
NARRATOR 1	In the grey early light, Ray snaps awake from his nightmare. As he lies in bed with his eyes open he realises that though the nightmare is over, the real life misery is still there.

Scene 15: In the kitchen, morning

(NARRATORS 1 and 2, MUM, RAY and ANNOUNCER)

NARRATOR 1   Ray is sitting at the table toying with his bowl of cereal. Derek is just finishing the last spoonful of his. Derek gets up and leaves the room as soon as he's finished.

NARRATOR 2   Ray's mother comes in with her bag and coat. She puts the coat over the back of a chair and starts to fumble in the bag. The local radio is playing music.

MUM   Eat up.

RAY   Not hungry.

MUM   You've got to eat something.
Do me a favour and buy a couple of pounds of sausages on your way back from school.
(*she lowers her voice*) I'm popping in to see Grandma after work. Don't say anything to Derek. I've told him she's had to go into hospital for a rest but I didn't say she was ill. It might upset him.

RAY   He'll be more upset if she dies and he didn't even know she was ill

MUM   Don't say things like that. You can make things happen, you know.

RAY   'Course you can't.

MUM   Anyway, I don't want anything said and that's an end to it.

14

NARRATOR 1	She begins to clear up the breakfast things. The local radio stops playing music. There's the station theme (From the land of the heart/To the heart of the land/Heartland radio). Mum turns up the radio.
ANNOUNCER	It's 8.0 o'clock here on Heartland Radio and the top news story this morning. Police are setting up a telephone hotline to help them with their investigation into a hit and run crash which resulted in the death of a sixty-three year old woman near the village of Blackston last night. Mrs Maureen Chalmers was killed when she was hit by a motorbike that had been stolen from Leshingham earlier in the evening.
MUM	Tt, how terrible.
ANNOUNCER	That hotline number for anyone who thinks they've got information that could help the police is Leshingham 33660.
NARRATOR 2	Ray has been listening horrified to this. As the very last bit is being read out, he gets up and heads for the door.
MUM	Don't forget the sausages.
ANNOUNCER	There was a lucky escape this morning for a Norester family whose house caught fire. Neighbours raised the alarm ...

Scene 16: School corridor, day

(NARRATORS 1 and 2, DAVE, RAY, IAN, JANE, BARBARA and MR HAWKS)

NARRATOR 1   A group of pupils is standing in the corridor waiting to go into the classroom. Ray is there, slightly apart, lost in his thoughts.

NARRATOR 2   Ray's friend, Dave, comes along the corridor. He stands next to Ray who doesn't notice him. Amused, Dave waves his hand in front of Ray's eyes.

DAVE   Miles away.

RAY   Hi.

NARRATOR 1   Dave grabs hold of Ray's head, one hand behind his neck, the other flat against his forehead.

DAVE   Don't tell me. I can read your thoughts.

NARRATOR 2   Ray struggles but Dave holds him captive. The others' attention is drawn to this little diversion.

RAY   Cut it out, Dave.

DAVE   Oh yes, this is one very worried man here. Yes, it's coming through to me – the secrets of your mind are revealed. Yes, here it is: When will people know the truth about me?

NARRATOR 1   Ray stops struggling, shaken by what Dave is saying.

DAVE	I'm a great footballer and Mr Raines ought to realise and pick me for the team today.
NARRATOR 2	Ray pushes him away. Dave laughs.
DAVE	He will. He will.
NARRATOR 1	Jane and Ian come along the corridor. Ian is humming the dead march.
IAN	Put your black armbands on, you lot.
JANE	It's not funny, Ian. We've just seen the caretaker putting the school flag down to half mast.
DAVE	What for?
JANE	The wife of one of the School Governors was killed in a motorbike crash last night.
BARBARA	Oh, I heard that on the news this morning.
MR HAWKS	Right, you can come in, now.

Scene 17: Classroom, day
(NARRATORS 1 and 2, JANE, MR HAWKS and RAY)

NARRATOR 1	Outside the classroom window a car draws up. Inside the classroom Ray and the others are working. Jane is sitting behind Ray. She looks out of the window and sees Mr Chalmers get out of the car and start towards the building. She nudges Ray.
JANE	That's Mr Chalmers – the guy whose wife was killed. Probably come to see the Head.

17

NARRATOR 2	Mr Hawks looks up from his marking.
MR HAWKS	Come on, Jane, get on with your work, please.
RAY	Can I be excused, Sir?
HAWKS	Yes.

Scene 18: School corridor, day
(NARRATORS 1 and 2, DOUGIE and RAY)

| NARRATOR 1 | Ray walks down a corridor and turns a corner. There, ahead of him, is Mr Chalmers sitting on a chair outside the Headmaster's office. Ray walks along towards him. Suddenly Mr Chalmers gets up and stands, looking down the corridor at him. It is, in fact, an entirely innocent moment for a man who is still reeling from the death of his wife. But it has a terrible effect on Ray as Mr Chalmers stares straight at him. |
| NARRATOR 2 | Ray's heart pounds as he approaches, then passes Mr Chalmers. He continues along the corridor. A door opens. The Headmaster comes out of this room. Ray stops and pretends to look at a notice board. He looks sideways along the corridor and sees the Head shake Mr Chalmer's hand and then put a comforting hand on his shoulder as he leads him back into his room. |

NARRATOR 1	Ray waits a moment, then moves back towards the Head's door. Cautiously he stops outside the door. He is about to put his ear to the door when a secretary comes out of the office next door and goes into another office down the corridor. She doesn't see him.
NARRATOR 2	Ray checks the corridor, then leans in to the door. There's only muffled voices to be heard. A hand comes down onto his shoulder and Ray spins round with a terrible gasp of fear. It is a fellow pupil, Dougie.
DOUGIE	What you up to?
RAY	Get stuffed, Dougie.
NARRATOR 1	Ray is blazing with fury and Dougie is startled by the reaction.
DOUGIE	What's up with you?
NARRATOR 2	Ray walks away...

Scene 19: School toilets, day
(NARRATORS 1 and 2)

NARRATOR 1	Ray is bending over a toilet, having just been sick. He coughs and gags, then straightens up and flushes the toilet.
NARRATOR 2	He comes out of the cubicle, turns on a tap, and runs water over his face. He looks at

himself in the mirror. He can't stop hearing the motorbike roar and the sound of the crash.

Scene 20: Classroom, day
(NARRATORS 1 and 2, MRS SCOTT, PATRICIA and RAY)

NARRATOR 1	Mrs Scott is standing in front of the class. She is holding the text book from which the class is working and is referring to a photo upon which the exercise is based.
MRS SCOTT	Patricia. Qu'est-ce qu'il fait, le petit garcon au bord du lac?
NARRATOR 2	Ray, book open, like the rest of the class, is wrapped in his thoughts of Mrs Chalmers' dead body in the road.
PATRICIA	Le garcon au bord de lac ...
MRS SCOTT	Du, du.
PATRICIA	... au bord du lac est en train de pecher.
MRS SCOTT	Bien, très bien. Ray. Est-ce qu'il a attrapé des poissons? Ray!
RAY	What? Pardon, Madame.
MRS SCOTT	Will you please pay attention.
NARRATOR 1	Ray glances at the book next to him and sees he has the wrong page. He starts to flip through the pages.
MRS SCOTT	Page cinquante six.

Scene 21: School corridor

(NARRATORS 1 and 2 and DAVE)

NARRATOR 1   It's the end of the school day. A scramble of boys are looking at the school teams which have been posted on the noticeboard. Dave and Ray are among them.

DAVE   Yeah! You've made it!

NARRATOR 2   Dave turns to Ray, grinning with pleasure. They slap hands as they make their way out of the melee. They go straight out of the door to the outside.

Scene 22: School drive

(NARRATORS 1 and 2, DAVE and RAY)

DAVE   Fantastic. I knew you'd make it.

RAY   It's only reserve.

DAVE   Only reserve. Yesterday you'd have killed for it. It's the school's top team, man. You've waited a whole year for this.

RAY   Yeah, it's great.

DAVE   You wait. With your luck I bet you Raines'll bring you on in the second half. You'll play a blinder and end up getting a permanent place in the team. Things always work out for you.

NARRATOR 1   Ray can't help but smile at Dave's enthusiasm. The smile stops as a police car

	turns in from the road and drives up to the school. They both stop and look.
DAVE	They've probably come about that accident.
NARRATOR 2	Two policemen get out of the car and go into the school. Dave and Ray turn and walk on.
RAY	Maybe . . . maybe they think someone at the school did it.
DAVE	Don't be daft. Even the nutters at this place wouldn't do something like that. Anyway, they'll never find out who did it.
RAY	Why?
DAVE	Aw, the cop's are useless. Nearly half the crimes that get done are never solved.
RAY	Is that true?
DAVE	'Course it is. Why d'you think people rob banks and stuff? 'Cause they know they're never gonna get caught. They wouldn't do it otherwise.
RAY	Less than half get caught?
DAVE	Yeah. I bet you they never catch that guy.
NARRATOR 1	They walk on. Ray breathes freer at Dave's news.

Scene 23: Kitchen, early evening

(NARRATORS 1 and 2, RAY and MUM)

NARRATOR 1	Mum is loading washing into the machine when Ray comes in.
RAY	How's Grandma?
NARRATOR 2	Mum stops loading and leans on the machine, her back to Ray. There's barely repressed anger in her voice.
MUM	She's so stubborn. I tried to tell her everything'll be all right but she just won't listen.
RAY	Maybe it won't be all right.
MUM	Now don't you start. She's going to be fine. I know she is. Doctors can do wonders nowadays.
NARRATOR 1	She starts loading the machine again and comes across Ray's torn jeans.
MUM	What on earth have you done to these?
NARRATOR 2	Ray tries to say what's torturing him.
RAY	Mum ..
MUM	What?
RAY	I had an accident.
MUM	I can see that. You are careless. We haven't got money to burn, you know.
NARRATOR 1	Ray would like to go on but the sight of her holding out the jeans accusingly stops him.

23

RAY	Can't they be patched?
MUM	Huh!
NARRATOR 2	She throws them into the machine.
NARRATOR 1	Ray would still like to find some way of saying what's on his mind.
RAY	I didn't do it on purpose. Accidents can happen, can't they?
MUM	Yes, if you're stupid or careless they can.
NARRATOR 2	She has now finished with the washing and moves to the fridge which she opens.
MUM	Where have you put the sausages?
RAY	Oh no ... I forgot them.
MUM	You what? What am I supposed to do for tea?
RAY	Mum, I'm sorry...
MUM	What good's 'sorry'? How could you forget? On top of everything...
NARRATOR 1	She's on the point of tears. Ray walks over to her and puts his hands on her shoulders.
RAY	Mum ... don't ...
NARRATOR 2	She shrugs his hands off her shoulders.
MUM	Don't think you can get round me like that.
RAY	Oh, for God's sake, it's only a few bloody sausages.

24

MUM	Don't you dare talk to me like that.
RAY	Oh, why don't you just shut up.
NARRATOR 1	Ray slams out of the kitchen.

Scene 24: Ray's bedroom, evening
(NARRATOR 1 and 2, DAD and RAY)

NARRATOR 1	Ray is lying on his bed. He's got a cassette player against one ear blaring out a rock guitar solo. The door opens and Dad comes in. Ray switches the tape off and sits up, avoiding his Dad's eyes.
DAD	What's all this, then?
NARRATOR 2	Ray shrugs.
DAD	What happened?
RAY	She freaked out about some sausages I forgot. She's always freaking out.
DAD	Ray, that's not true and you know it.
RAY	She just . . . thinks you can't make mistakes sometimes. I mean if she freaks out about sausages. . . . And she acts as if everything'll be OK if you think it's OK. As if you can . . . just make problems go away or something.
DAD	What problems?
RAY	Anything. I don't know . . . Grandma. I

mean, why doesn't she tell Derek instead of all this stupid pretending?

DAD   Well, I think he ought to know as well.

RAY   Well, why don't you tell him?

NARRATOR 1   Dad shrugs weakly.

DAD   It would only upset your Mum. You know what she's like. And she's got a lot on her mind at the moment.

RAY   Yeah? Well, so have I.

DAD   What? Tell me.

NARRATOR 2   Ray looks into his father's eyes and longs to tell him. But he can't.

RAY   I don't know. Exams. All sorts of things.

DAD   What?

RAY   Things. I got picked for the football team.

DAD   Ray, that's great. When, tomorrow? That's great. We'll have to come and watch. Oh, well done. Oh come on, don't let a silly row spoil all that. Why not just say sorry to Mum and clear the air? Eh? That's my boy.

Scene 25: The kitchen, evening
(NARRATORS 1 and 2, RAY, MUM, DAD and DEREK)

NARRATOR 1   Ray and Dad come in. Mum and Derek are sitting at the table. Ray goes up to Mum and kisses her on the cheek.

RAY	I'm sorry.
MUM	That's all right, love. I'm sorry, too. Anyway, your Dad's been to get some fish and chips.
DAD	Yes, and Ray gets extra fish to build him up. He's been picked for the football team tomorrow.
MUM	Oh Ray! That's wonderful.
NARRATOR 2	Dad is getting the fish and chips out of the oven.
DAD	Just think, in a few years when he's a big soccer star we'll all be living in luxury.
NARRATOR 1	They all laugh and cheer. Ray smiles with pleasure.
DEREK	You'll have to play for United. Yeah! U-nited! You'll be on telly.
MUM	You and telly, that's all you think about.
DAD	Ooh, these plates are hot!
MUM	Can you get the vinegar, Derek?
NARRATOR 2	While the rest of the family have been talking, an irresistible but terrible idea has been dawning an Ray.
RAY	I think I'll go out on my bike after the meal. Do a last bit of training for tomorrow.

Scene 26: Site of the accident, night

(NARRATORS 1 and 2, RAY and INSPECTOR)

NARRATOR 1	Ray is riding his bike on the Blackston Road. He stops abruptly, staring at something. It's a police notice asking for information from anybody who saw the accident that took place on Thursday 6th Feb at 8.30pm. Ray puts his bike down on the ground and walks over to the spot where Mrs Chalmers' Mini stood. There's a scrunching underfoot and he sees fragments of glass. Ray closes his eyes, shaking his head in contrition.
RAY	I'm sorry. Please hear me, Mrs Chalmers. I'm sorry.
NARRATOR 2	Ray opens his eyes. There's a sound and he looks round. Nothing. Suddenly, with a loud clunk, a bright light beams down on him, illuminating him in a glaring white pool of light. A police inspector in uniform walks into the bean of light. His manner is kindly.
INSPECTOR	We've been waiting for you, son. You know what they say: a murderer always comes back to the scene of the crime.
NARRATOR 2	Ray turns his head. Mum, Dad and Derek are standing in the circle of light, looking at him.

NARRATOR 1   The light switches off. Ray is alone on the empty road. The wind rustles the trees. A cold moon looks down. The noise of the wind grows louder round Ray as he stands forlornly in the moonlight.

ACT TWO

Scene 1: Dream sequence
(NARRATORS 1 and 2 and INSPECTOR)

NARRATOR 1   It is night at the crash site. Mrs Chalmers'
              car is parked, the door wide open. She is
              lying dead in the road. A police inspector is
              bending down next to the motorbike,
              brushing powder onto the handlebars.

INSPECTOR   All we have to do is fingerprint the whole
              school and we'll get him.

NARRATOR 2   Ray runs in agonising slow motion along a
              school corridor. It is night and behind him
              down the corridor a group of torch beams
              flash towards him. A light flashes in his
              face. He holds up his hands to cover his
              face.

NARRATOR 1   Ray, in slow motion, runs up some stairs in
              the school. He gets to the top and opens
              the door.

NARRATOR 2   The scene changes. Ray is near a church.
              The door swings open and Ray steps in. He
              looks towards the altar.

NARRATOR 1   There is a huge blaze of flames like hell
              burning.

NARRATOR 2   Ray is on his knees in an empty pew. He
              looks straight ahead. He closes his eyes in

an attempt at prayer. He opens his eyes. He turns his head. The dead Mrs Chalmers is sitting in the pew next to him.

Scene 2: Hallway, day

(NARRATORS 1 and 2, DAD and RAY)

NARRATOR 1	Ray comes down the stairs. His dad appears in the doorway of the sitting room, and beckons him into the room.
DAD	Ray.
NARRATOR 2	Ray imagines what his father will say: 'We've found out what you've done.'
NARRATOR 1	Ray goes into the sitting room. His Dad is waiting.
DAD	Listen, Ray, I'm afraid we won't be able to come and watch you play this afternoon.
RAY	Why?
DAD	We're going to have to go to the hospital. Grandma's really ill. I mean *really*. I'm sure she'd love to see you; you know how fond she is of you. Perhaps you could go tomorrow.
RAY	Yeah, sure.
DAD	Anyway, I'm sorry to miss the game.
RAY	I'm only reserve anyway.

DAD	Whatever. I'd have liked to see you. I'm really proud of you, you know. I couldn't ask for a better son than you.
NARRATOR 2	Ray smiles with pleasure as his Dad gives his shoulder a little squeeze. Then he hears the sound of the motorbike crash, police sirens, and the distant voice of his mother screaming, 'Ray, what have you done?'

Scene 3: Football pitch, day

(NARRATORS 1 and 2, MR RAINES, RAY, CAPTAIN, REF, DAVE and CHRIS)

NARRATOR 1	Ray and Mr Raines are on the touchline watching the game. There is also the trainer from the other school and a few pupils and parents who've come to support.
NARRATOR 2	Ray's team, Vermont High, is on the defence as the opposition, Harrison Road, move towards goal spearheaded by a winger who goes past two Vermont defenders and gets in an excellent cross. A forward connects with the ball but it sails past the goalpost for a goalkick.
MR RAINES	Come on, Vermont High, don't lose it in the last few minutes.
NARRATOR 1	Raines turns to Ray.
MR RAINES	Get your tracksuit off. Dougie's looking tired and I want some fresh legs to stop that number 7.

NARRATOR 2	Ray begins to take off his tracksuit. Raines attracts the referee and indicates that he wants to make a substitution.
MR RAINES	Ref! Dougie. It's up to you, Ray. Don't let that number 7 get past you. Firm, but nothing dirty. Right?
NARRATOR 1	Ray goes out onto the pitch. The departing Dougie pats him on the shoulder.
NARRATOR 2	Ray takes up his position. The throw-in takes place. The Harrison player who gets the ball starts an attack. Ray moves in towards him but the ball goes through his legs. He tries to recover but trips and fall. Ray gets up quickly but feels humiliated. He looks over at Mr Raines who makes fists of 'come on' at him.
NARRATOR 1	A long through ball cuts open the Harrison defence and Dave runs on to the pass and heads for goal. The goalkeeper tips it away for a corner. The corner is taken but the Harrison goalkeeper rises high and catches it. Ray immediately starts to run back to get into a defensive position. As he does so, the Harrison goalkeeper boots the ball upfield.
NARRATOR 2	Ray and a Harrison winger, H7, charge towards the ball. It's going to be close but H7 gets there first. Ray launches a furious sliding tackle. His foot takes the ball and then smashes H7 on the shin.

NARRATOR 1	Ray gets up and looks down at H7 lying motionless on the ground. For a moment, it is not H7 that Ray is seeing, but Mrs Chalmers dead on the road.
NARRATOR 2	H7 rolls over, holding on to his shin. Ray offers his hand to help him up.
RAY	Are you Ok? I'm sorry.
H7	Oh yeah, I bet you are.
NARRATOR 1	There's some booing from the crowd. The Harrison captain now rounds on the Ref.
CAPTAIN	What you going to do about it, Ref?
REF	It was a 50/50 ball. Looked a fair tackle to me.
CAPTAIN	You're joking. He went for the player. He's a bloody thug.
REF	Watch your language, son, or you'll be the one who ends up in the book. Throw in to Harrison.
CAPTAIN	Ref.
REF	Throw in.
NARRATOR 2	The Harrison team is reluctant but the Ref points to the touch and the game starts again. Ray jogs back towards a defensive position. He can hear what Raines said earlier, 'Firm, but nothing dirty, right?'
NARRATOR 1	Play continues for awhile and then the Ref blows 'time'.

NARRATOR 2	The players wander off the pitch. Ray walks towards Mr Raines who is just turning away from the Harrison trainer.
RAY	Is he OK?
MR RAINES	He'll live.
RAY	I'm really sorry about . . .
MR RAINES	I've nothing to say, lad. The Ref judged the tackle fair, so fair it is as far as I'm concerned. If the truth is any different, it's on your conscience, not mine. Anyway, you played well.
NARRATOR 1	Ray turns to join the others heading for the changing rooms. Dave comes up and puts his arm round Ray's shoulder. Chris joins them.
DAVE	Well done, mate. That tackle! Well wicked. Only saved the game for us. I told you you'd play well. You can celebrate at the party tonight.
CHRIS	Yeah, we'll get well tanked up.

Scene 4: The party, night
(NARRATORS 1 and 2, DAVE, RAY, JANE and ANNA)

NARRATOR 1	The soccer team and a whole group of their friends are celebrating the victory. Music is playing, couples are dancing, people are eating and drinking. Ray is standing in the

dark, alone, with a can of strong lager in this hand. He's watching a couple of girls – Anna and Jane – who are dancing. Anna sees him and smiles. He smiles back. He takes a sip of beer. Dave comes by and stops.

DAVE   Go on, get in there. Don't act innocent – I saw you smiling at each other.

RAY   Shut up, Dave.

DAVE   I don't get you. You are the luckiest bloke I know and you never go for things.

RAY   What do you mean – lucky?

DAVE   You're lucky. Things always work out for you. You could get away with murder. So take advantage. Get in there. She's yours for the asking, randy git.

NARRATOR 2   Ray laughs in embarrassment and pushes Dave who, rather drunkenly, goes on his way. Ray looks again at Anna.

NARRATOR 1   Suddenly, he gets a flash-back to the crash. Upset that the memory haunts him even here, he raises the lager can and downs the rest.

NARRATOR 2   Ray goes into the kitchen where he sees a bottle of vodka. He takes a paper cup, pours a large measure of vodka and downs it in one go. He doesn't like it, but what the hell?

DAVE	Boozer! How many of those have you had?
RAY	Six. And some vodka.
DAVE	You must be more out of your skull than I am.
RAY	Dave, you're my friend, aren't you?
DAVE	'Course I am.
RAY	Would you tell me if you were in trouble?
DAVE	'Course I would. Why? Aha, you're planning to get into trouble with that Anna Hartfield aren't you?
RAY	No.
DAVE	Yes, you are. I can tell. Listen, I've just been talking to Jane and she says that Anna only came here tonight 'cos you were going to be here.
RAY	Get off.
DAVE	It's true. I swear. Look, come on, Ray, she's yours. Things don't happen by chance, you know. You gotta make them happen.
RAY	'Course things happen by chance. That's why I'm in the mess I'm in.
DAVE	You're in the mess you're in 'cos you've drunk too much. Come on. Anna's waiting.
NARRATOR 1	Dave pulls Ray back to the main party room.

DAVE	Anna! Anna! Anna, this is my friend Ray, Ray, this is my friend, Anna. And this is her friend, Jane. Jane, meet my friend . . .
JANE	Don't be stupid, Dave, we're in the same Maths set.
NARRATOR 2	Dave looks at Ray and makes 'go on' signs with his eyes.
DAVE	Well?
RAY	Shut up, will you.
DAVE	God, you're hopeless. Anna, would you like to dance with Ray? Yes. Ray, would you like to dance with Anna? Yes. Then dance.
NARRATOR 1	Ray and Anna look at each other and agree.
RAY	I've seen you around with Jane.
ANNA	Yeah, I've seen you.
RAY	You wait for her after school.
ANNA	Yeah. I go to St Greg's. We get out earlier than you, so I wait for her. She said you'd be here.
RAY	Oh?
ANNA	Yeah.
RAY	This didn't happen by chance, then?
ANNA	What d'you mean?
RAY	Nothing.

38

NARRATOR 2	While they've been talking slow music has started. Ray moves in closer to Anna and they start to sway. Suddenly Anna puts her arms round him and pulls him tight. The warmth and security of someone's arms is exactly what Ray has needed and he clasps her tight, pressing his face into her hair.

Scene 5: Outside the party, night
(NARRATORS 1 and 2, RAY and ANNA)

NARRATOR 1	Ray and Anna are standing at the side of the house.
ANNA	I knew.
RAY	What?
ANNA	That I'd like you.
RAY	You don't know me.
ANNA	I like what I know.
RAY	What about what you don't know? I could be anything. I could've done all sorts of things.
NARRATOR 2	Anna pulls him close and kisses him. There's the slam of a car door. A policeman in uniform comes up the path to the house. Ray breaks from Anna and pulls her towards the back garden, indicating her to be quiet. When they get to the garden he lets go.
ANNA	What's going on?

RAY	A cop's just turned up.
ANNA	Must be my dad. He said he'd pick me up when he got off duty.
RAY	He's a cop?
ANNA	Yeah, why? You're not a criminal, are you? I'll have to go. Phone me. The number's in the book. Hartfield. 16 Princes Close. How about tomorrow afternoon?
RAY	I've got to go and see my Grandma in hospital.
ANNA	Well just ring sometime. I gotta go.
NARRATOR 1	She kisses Ray, then runs into the house by the back door. Ray leans against the wall and slides down into a crouch. He's drunk, confused. He can hear the noise of the crash. Ray cups his head in his hands.

Scene 6: Back at the party

(NARRATORS 1 and 2, DOUGIE, IAN and RAY)

NARRATOR 1	Ray comes in to the crowded room. Dougie is standing talking to Ian. As Ray walks past he sways into Dougie's back
DOUGIE	Oh, oh watch out, it's the killer.
IAN	How you doing, killer?
DOUGIE	Raines takes me off; me a player of skill and finesse; and he sends the hard man into action. Two minutes later, one dead winger.

NARRATOR 2	They laugh. It's a harmless tease but the effect on Ray is terrible.
RAY	Just shut up, will you. The ref said the tackle was fair. Just shut up.
NARRATOR 1	Ray turns and lurches out of the room.
DAVE	Hey, man, where you going?

Scene 7: The street, night
(NARRATOR 1 and RAY)

NARRATOR 1	Ray walks down the street, swaying and on the point of tears. He stands in the road gripped by the misery, raises his arms, clenches his fists and howls.
RAY	Help me!

Scene 8: Bathroom, the next day
(NARRATORS 1 and 2, DEREK and RAY)

NARRATOR 1	Ray splashes water on his face and looks at his tongue. He feels terrible. He opens the bathroom cabinet and sees his Dad's razor. He takes it out. He opens it up and takes out the blade. He bunches one fist and exposes his wrist, then brings the blade closer and closer to the vein. There's a knock on the door.
DEREK	Ray. Ray.

41

RAY	What?
DEREK	You coming down? Mum and Dad've been out for hours. I've been on my own. I've been waiting for you to get up. Ray? I'll make you a cup of tea if you want.
NARRATOR 2	Ray looks at the razor in his fingers and drops it.
RAY	OK. I'll be down in a minute.

Scene 9: Sitting room, day
(NARRATORS 1 and 2, DEREK and RAY)

NARRATOR 1	Derek is sitting watching the TV when Ray comes in. The young boy's face lights up.
DEREK	Hello.
NARRATOR 2	Ray slumps down on the sofa. Derek gets up and sits down next to his brother. Derek punches Ray affectionately. Ray punches him back.
RAY	Where've Mum and Dad gone?
DEREK	To see Grandma. There's your tea. I put the sugar in.
NARRATOR 1	Ray ruffles Derek's hair.
RAY	You're a star.
DEREK	I want to come and see you play football next time.

42

RAY	If I get picked.
DEREK	You will – you're great. Dad couldn't get the car started this morning because of the plugs. We had to push it.
NARRATOR 2	They both look at the TV for a few minutes.
RAY	What's happened?
DEREK	That boy stole some money from school, but he wrote a letter that made it look like someone else did it. So everybody blames it on another boy that nobody likes because his dad's poor and they live in a hut. There – that one with the red hair.

Scene 10: Ray's bedroom, day
(NARRATORS 1 and 2 and RAY)

NARRATOR 1	Ray is at his desk which is piled high with cut-up newspapers. He is wearing rubber gloves and is cutting out a large letter 'T'. He completes the cutting, puts glue on the back and sticks it on a piece of paper to complete a word.
NARRATOR 2	Ray holds up the finished note. He reads it softly to himself.
RAY	'I killed Mrs Chalmers. I have decided to commit suicide because the disgrace will kill my wife.' That'll put them off the scent.

NARRATOR 1	Ray folds the note and slips it into an envelope marked 'City Police, Leshingham'.
NARRATOR 2	As he seals the envelope he hears Dave's voice echoing in his head: 'You're lucky. Things always work out for you. You could get away with murder.'

Scene 11: Ray's bedroom, day
(NARRATORS 1 and 2 and DAD)

NARRATOR 1	Ray is folding the last of the newspapers after tidying his room. He puts the pile neatly on his bed. There is the sound of a car horn being blown urgently. Ray goes to the window and opens it.
NARRATOR 2	His parents' car is outside. It is raining. His Mum has just closed the passenger door and is scurrying in to the house. His Dad is at the driving wheel and calls through the open car window.
DAD	This damn thing's playing up so I daren't stop the engine. If you want a lift to the hospital you'd better come now. Hurry up.
NARRATOR 1	Ray quickly closes the window. He races to the door, grabs his parka and rushes out of the room.
NARRATOR 2	On the desk lies the sealed envelope.

Scene 12: Outside the hospital

(NARRATOR 1, DAD and RAY)

NARRATOR 1   Ray is sitting in the car next to his dad. It is
             raining. They pull up outside the hospital.
             His dad pulls out some money and hands
             Ray £5.

DAD   There's no guarantee I'll be able to get the
             car started again when I get home, so I
             think you'd better catch a bus back. OK?

RAY   I've got money.

DAD   Take it. See you later.

Scene 13: Hospital corridor

(NARRATORS 1 and 2, VOICE, RAY and ANNA)

NARRATOR 1   Ray is dialling a number on a public
             payphone. A telephone directory is open in
             front of him and he checks the number as
             he dials. The number begins to ring. The
             phone is answered – we hear a man's voice:

VOICE   Hello.

RAY   Can I speak to Anna Hartfield please?

VOICE   Who shall I say it is?

RAY   Tell her it's Ray. Say we met at the party
             last night.

VOICE   Hold on.

NARRATOR 2	Ray covers up the receiver and practises while waiting for Anna to come to the phone.
RAY	Hi! I wondered if you'd like to come out with me. Hi! It was great to meet you last night. Hi! Did you get home OK? Hi! I said I'd ring – so I am.
NARRATOR 1	As he rehearses this last phrase, Ray idly looks at the things on the wall. Suddenly his eye is drawn to a photo with the caption 'Friends of Leshingham Hospital'. There, among the others stand Mr and Mrs Chalmers. At this moment the phone is picked up at the other end by Anna.
ANNA	Hello. Hello? Ray? Is anyone there? Hello. Ray?
NARRATOR 2	Ray puts the phone down.

Scene 14: Hospital room

(NARRATORS 1 and 2, RAY, GRANDMA and NURSE)

NARRATOR 1	Grandma is lying in bed. She is not in a ward but it's a mean little room.
NARRATOR 2	Ray is sitting by her side. He's been making an effort to cheer her up – telling her what he's been doing – and he's succeeded. It's obvious that they really like each other. Grandma is chuckling as he reaches the end of the story.

RAY	Anyway, then her dad arrived so she had to go home. Then I left, too, I haven't the faintest idea how I got home. And this morning my head felt about that big.
GRANDMA	Oh you are wicked, Ray, getting drunk at your age.
RAY	Wicked? Do you think I am?
GRANDMA	Oh we all do silly things when we're young. Mustn't let drinking become a habit, though.
RAY	I wouldn't dare tell Mum and Dad about getting drunk. Sometimes I think if they knew what I was really like ... They still think I'm just a good little kid.
GRANDMA	Instead of a wicked grown-up who gets drunk and goes out to parties with girls. What's her name?
RAY	Anna.
GRANDMA	Oh, I'm so sleepy. It's those pills they give me.
RAY	Grandma, do you believe in fate?
GRANDMA	What do you mean?
RAY	Well, supposing I went out of here and a brick fell on my head or I got knocked down by a car. Well, do you think that something like that happens because it was meant to happen, and there's no way of stopping it?

GRANDMA	I really don't know, Ray. But I do think that . . . there are some things you just can't run away from. That's your mother's problem – she hasn't learned yet that there are certain things in life that you just have to accept. Like dying. She was in a bit of a state when she left here this morning.
RAY	I didn't see her. The car's playing up so I came out in a rush.
GRANDMA	I'm so sleepy. It's important, Ray.
RAY	What is?
NARRATOR 1	But she has slipped into sleep. Ray strokes her hand. Then he leans forward and whispers.
RAY	Grandma. Grandma.
NARRATOR 2	She doesn't respond.
RAY	In the football game I told you about. That tackle. It wasn't true what I said. I knew I couldn't get the ball so I went for him.
NARRATOR 1	Grandma still doesn't respond. Ray lowers his voice still more.
RAY	Grandma? I stole a bike. I don't even know why I did it.
NARRATOR 2	Grandma still doesn't respond. Ray moves in closer.
RAY	Grandma. I've killed someone. It was an

accident. But I don't know what to do. Mum and Dad . . .

NARRATOR 1   Ray's nightmare returns. He is holding out his blood stained hands while his mother wails.

RAY   Grandma. What can I do?

NARRATOR 2   As he is whispering to her, a hand taps Ray on the shoulder. He jumps. A male nurse is there.

NURSE   I should let her sleep if I were you.

NARRATOR 1   Ray nods. He gets up, then bends down and kisses her cheek. He turns and walks away.

Scene 15: Bus shelter

(NARRATORS 1 and 2, MRS FITZROY, RAY and CONDUCTOR)

NARRATOR 1   Ray is standing at a bus shelter with various other people. He is lost in thought. A bus approaches. It pulls up and the passengers get ready to board. There's a voice behind Ray.

MRS FITZROY   Ray! Hello.

RAY   Hello Mrs Fitzroy.

MRS FITZROY   Fancy seeing you here. Have you been visiting?

RAY   Yes, my Grandma.

NARRATOR 2	The passengers shuffle forward to the bus.
MRS FITZROY	Oh, I'm sorry to hear that.
NARRATOR 1	As Ray steps on to the bus, the conductor turns. It's the same one as on the fateful night. They look in each other's eyes.
NARRATOR 2	Ray is frozen. The conductor is not quite sure. Mrs Fitzroy taps Ray from behind.
MRS FITZROY	Come on, Ray. What's up?
NARRATOR 1	Ray ducks his head and starts forward. The conductor takes Ray's arm.
CONDUCTOR	Don't I know you? You're the boy from the other night, aren't you?
NARRATOR 2	Ray breaks from the conductor's grasp, pushing him off balance so that the conductor sprawls into the aisle. Ray pushes past Mrs Fitzroy and jumps off the bus.
MRS FITZROY	Ray! Ray!
NARRATOR 1	Ray bursts across the road, narrowly missing being knocked down by a car. The conductor gets up and starts off the bus after Ray but realises that he can't make up the lost ground, especially as the traffic is flowing. He turns back to the bus and sees Mrs Fitzroy.
CONDUCTOR	Do you know where he lives? He's the one the police want to talk to about that accident the other night.

50

Scene 16: Back alley

(NARRATORS 1 and 2)

NARRATOR 1   Ray dodges round a corner, runs across the street and keeps running.

NARRATOR 2   He ducks into an alley and runs along it, jumping the puddles and ruts past the garages. He stops. He looks behind him, sees there's no one pursuing him and dodges into an empty garage. He leans against the wall totally out of breath. He slides down and hunches into a ball.

NARRATOR 1   His head is bursting with memories of:
the bike ride,
Mrs Chalmers death,
the first nightmare,
Grandma,
the party,
the conductor,
these all begin to spin round and round in his mind.

NARRATOR 2   An hour passes. It is dark in the garage now. A car bumps along the alley. It turns in towards the garage. Its headlights light up the interior and the driver stops the car as he makes out the form of Ray. Ray gets up and runs out past the car and away.

Scene 17: Cinema, night

(NARRATORS 1 and 2, ACTRESS, ACTOR, DAD, RAY and MUM)

NARRATOR 1 — Ray is asleep in his seat at the cinema. He is worn out by the running and the tension. Suddenly there's dramatic music and the sound of a car chase on the screen. A loud explosion wakes Ray up. He sits up and looks at the screen. There's the sound of a single gunshot.

ACTRESS — Is he dead?

ACTOR — Yes.

ACTRESS — What am I going to do?

ACTOR — Just stick to your story. It's your word against his. You may be as guilty as hell but if you say it's all a mistake, and you keep on saying it; they won't be able to prove a thing.

ACTRESS — And will you be there with me?

ACTOR — Do you have to ask? Look in my eyes. I said, look in my eyes.

NARRATOR 2 — Ray gets up and heads for the foyer where there's a phone booth. He goes inside and starts dialling his parents' number.

DAD — Hello? Ray? Ray is that you? Please say something, Ray.

RAY — It's me, Dad.

DAD — Oh thank God.

DAD	(*to Ray's mum*) He's safe.
MUM	Ray! Oh Ray!
DAD	Ray . . . the police are here.
RAY	I know. But listen, I can explain everything. It's all a mistake.
DAD	I knew it. I couldn't believe what they were saying. Oh thank God. Ray . . . we thought you were dead.
RAY	What?
DAD	They found this note that said . . . you were going to kill yourself.
NARRATOR 1	Ray remembers the note – especially the words 'I killed Mrs Chalmers'. He realises that he can't bluff his way out of that. The phone slips from his hand and he walks out of the booth.
DAD	Ray. Ray. Are you there? What's happened? Ray. Please say something.

Scene 18: Train station, night
(NARRATOR 1 and GRANDMA'S VOICE)

NARRATOR 1	Ray is standing at the departures board. It spins to show 'London St. Pancras'.
GRANDMA'S VOICE	There are some things you just can't run away from.

Scene 19: Hallway, night

(NARRATOR 1, DAD and RAY)

NARRATOR 1   Ray's Dad is standing outside the sitting
              room door. He is waiting, hoping that the
              phone will ring. He looks in to the sitting
              room where the policeman is sitting
              dutifully looking at Mum who is slumped
              in a chair, her hands over her face. Dad
              starts to walk towards the kitchen. The
              phone begins to ring and he runs back to
              pick it up.

DAD   Hello? Ray? Please don't ring off. It doesn't
              matter what you've done. Just
              don't . . . don't . . . hurt yourself.

RAY   Dad, I didn't mean that about . . . killing
              myself. I'm sorry.

DAD   And the other stuff . . . about Mrs.
              Chalmers?

RAY   That's true. The stuff about the accident's
              true.

DAD   It doesn't matter. We can sort it out. I'm
              sure it wasn't your fault.

RAY   Don't say that. It *was* my fault. I know
              that. It *was*.

DAD   It doesn't matter.

DAD   Ray, please come home.

RAY   Dad.

DAD	Yes.
RAY	I keep thinking about Mrs Chalmers sitting in that car waiting. And me on the bike. Coming down the road. Getting closer and closer. And I wonder... if it's been like that for years. The two of us living our lives, never meeting but getting closer and closer to that moment when... Dad, stay there. I'm coming home.

Drama activities

1   Divide into groups of four. Read the party scenes from page 35 to page 41 again.

   • Set up two still pictures, (like 'freeze frames' from a video), of what you think are the most important moments from the party.
   • Try to show how Ray is feeling, and how others at the party react to him.
   • Each person in the group plays a character at the party, and no words or movement are allowed.
   • You can change which characters are in each of the 'freeze frames', but the same person will need to play Ray in each picture.
   • Practise going from one still picture to the next as smoothly as you can, and remember to show the other characters' attitudes to Ray.
   • Now add a spoken title to each picture. One of the characters in the picture can speak the title as the picture is 'frozen'.
   • Prepare your pictures for about fifteen minutes, and then each group shows their 'freeze frames' to the rest of the class.
   • Discuss why you chose those moments, and why you thought they were the most important.

2   In pairs, discuss what you think will happen to Ray after he gives himself up.

   • Will he be sent for trial?
   • Will he be sent to prison or remand home?
   • How long will any sentence be?

   Then imagine a situation in which Ray returns to his home and school after he has seen the police or served a sentence. One person in your group is Ray, the other is any of the following characters: Mum or Dad; Mr Chalmers; any of his friends from school; Grandma; Mr Raines.

- What might happen at their first meeting after the trial and sentence?
- How would they feel about each other?
- Would there be any bitterness or resentment?
- Would the characters from the play want to avoid Ray?
- Would they try to help him?

Try acting out the scene as it might happen.

Writing and talking about the play

1 The two narrators in the play help us to picture the action of the play as it is going on, as if we were watching a film. Choose a section of the play that is particularly dependent on the action – say from Ray stealing the motorbike to his running away – and draw a film 'storyboard' version of the action.

Think carefully about the picture that you would like to see in each frame and write a few words besides each frame to explain your ideas.

2 Imagine that you are the detective in charge of the CID investigation of the hit and run killing of Mrs Chalmers. Work with a group to look carefully at the play for the kinds of evidence that might be available to you. Divide the play between you to look for evidence.

Write a report of what the detective and his team discover up to the point that they find Ray's letter. You can include statements of all the characters interviewed as well as the picture they have built up about the 'killer'.

3 In this play, we know that Ray has killed Mrs Chalmers. When other characters say or do certain things, it has an effect on Ray that only he and the audience know about. This helps us to identify more with Ray, as the main character and appreciate how he is feeling. This is called *dramatic irony.*

There are examples on page 18, when by chance, Ray sees Mr Chalmers in school; on page 40, when Dougie and Ian call Ray 'killer'. Only Ray and the audience know how right they are.

Read through these scenes and discuss what effect this has on Ray, and also, the effect it has upon you, the audience.

4 *Collision Course* is a kind of modern tragedy. Ray brings about his own downfall, partly by his own actions and partly because of the workings of Fate.

Discuss in groups, how far the death of Mrs Chalmers was Ray's fate and how far it was Ray's own fault.

You can take the ideas from your discussion as starting point for a piece of writing in the style of a feature article for the local newspaper, under the headline 'Teenage motorcycle killer – mindless yob or innocent victim?'

5 Write a poem called 'Collision Course'. Try to capture the idea that somehow Ray and Mrs Chalmers were somehow meant to collide. Write alternate stanzas; one about Mrs Chalmers leaving her house and then a similar one about Ray and so on. Look closely at the narrators' speeches to help build up some ideas for lines and images for the poem.

PUBLISHED BY BBC EDUCATIONAL PUBLISHING AND
LONGMAN GROUP LIMITED

BBC Educational Publishing
a division of
BBC Enterprises Limited
Woodlands
80 Wood Lane
London W12 0TT

Pearson Education Limited
Edinburgh Gate,
Harlow,
Essex,
CM20 2JE
England, and Associated
Companies throughout the
World

Text of play © Nigel Hinton 1992 based on
the book *Collision Course* © Nigel Hinton
1976, 1983

This educational edition © BBC Enterprises Limited/Longman Group UK
Limited 1992

*All rights reserved; no part of this publication
may be reproduced, stored in a retrieval system,
or transmitted in any form or by any means, electronic,
mechanical, photocopying, recording, or otherwise,
without either the prior written permission of the
Publishers or a licence permitting restricted copying
issued by the Copyright Licensing Agency Ltd, 90 Tottenham
Court Road, London W1P 9HE.*

**This educational edition first published 1992
Fifteenth impression 2006**

ISBN-10: 0-582-09555-7
ISBN-13: 978-0-582-09555-7

Cover photograph © Roger Tonge
Printed in Malaysia, PP